Saturated in the Light and Life of Christ

a study on devotion to Jesus from the book of john

Judy Halmrast

Saturated in the Light and Life of Christ:

a study on devotion to Jesus from the book of john

Copyright © 2015 Judy Halmrast

All rights reserved.

No portion of this book may be reproduced, stored in a retrieval system, or transmitted in any form or by any means—electronic, mechanical, photocopy, recording, scanning, or other—without the prior permission of the author.

ISBN:1519209576
ISBN-13:9781519209573

Scripture quotations are taken from the Holy Bible, New International Version, NIV. Copyright © 1978 by New York International Bible Society

"In Him was life, and that life was the light of men."

JOHN 1:4

DISCIPLESHIP IS BASED NOT ON DEVOTION TO ABSTRACT IDEALS, BUT ON DEVOTION TO A PERSON, THE LORD JESUS CHRIST.

--OSWALD CHAMBERS

CONTENTS

	Background and Introduction to the Book of John	1
1	Lesson 1: Light and Life - *John 1:1-18*	2
2	Lesson 2: Unveiling Jesus - *John 1:19-3:36*	8
3	Lesson 3: Encountering Christ – *John 4-5*	14
4	Lesson 4: Food for Life – *John 6-7*	21
5	Lesson 5: Called to Live in Light – *John 8-9*	29
6	Lesson 6: Called to Live in Life – *John 10-11*	36
7	Lesson 7: Devotion Poured Out – *John 12-13*	43
8	Lesson 8 and 9: The Heart of Devoted Discipleship – *John 14-17*	50
9	Lesson 10: Life Unending – *John 18-21*	63

Background and Introduction to the Book of John

The Author
John, the writer of this fourth gospel, was one of Jesus' original 12 disciples and part of Jesus' inner circle of three (Peter, James, and John). He had a very close relationship with Jesus and is believed by many to be Jesus' closest friend. Jesus entrusted to John the care of his mother after his death. John and his brother James were the sons of Zebedee—fishermen by trade—and given the name "sons of Thunder" by Jesus in the gospel of Luke. John lived the longest of the original 12 disciples and also authored 1,2,3 John and the book of Revelation.

The Book
The book of John was written in approximately 80-90 A.D., about 50 years after John witnessed Jesus' earthly ministry. One does not have to read more than the first sentence of this gospel to realize that it is rather different than the other gospels. Indeed, as commentator Matthew Henry states, "He (John) gives us more of the mystery of that which the other evangelists (or gospel writers) gave us only the history." He continues, "The other evangelists wrote more of the bodily things of Christ; but John writes of the spiritual things of the gospel, the life and soul of it."*

A Note about the Study
Because the Bible is God's living and active Word, there are probably an infinite number of ways a person could approach this great book and be forever changed. The goal of this particular study is to encourage you, the reader, in a growing and intimate relationship with Jesus Christ and to spur you on in your devotion to Him. Light and life are themes throughout the book of John: Jesus *is* light and life and he *offers* light and life to all. It is through this thematic lens that we will approach our study. As we walk through the entire book of John, we will pay particular attention to this theme in Jesus' encounters with individuals and in His direct teaching. Like the apostle John, when we are saturated with the light and life of Christ, our response can be nothing less than increasingly devoting our lives to Him.

The study is broken down into 10 lessons. For the sake of organization, each lesson is divided into homework for that day, as noted in the study (e.g., "Day 1").

---

*Matthew Henry's Commentary, Zondervan Publishers, 1961.
Other resources:
John: The Gospel of Life, by Gary M. Burge, Zondervan Publishers, 2008.
The MacArthur Bible Commentary, by John MacArthur, Thomas Nelson Publishing, 2005.

Light and Life
Lesson 1
Introduction: John 1:1–18

A book's introduction has enormous potential to set the tone for the entire story. Words of suspense, whimsy, or practicality often draw us into the journey and give us a foretaste of what is yet to come. Take these familiar lead sentences in a book's introduction for example:

"It was the best of times; it was the worst of times...."*
"In a hole in the ground there lived a hobbit...."**

This is, of course, intentionally designed by the author.

So, too, does the introduction to the book of John establish the tenor for the remaining 21 chapters John will pen. Carefully, thoughtfully, and beautifully crafted, verses 1-18 form the powerful and artistic introduction to the book of John.

Day 1

1. Read John 1:1-18, taking time to let the beauty, imagery, and profundity of this text wash over you.

2. Read Matthew 1:1-16, Mark 1:1-8, and Luke 1:1-4. How is John's introduction different from that of the other three gospels'?

Days 2-4

1. Read John 1:1-18 again. You will notice several words used repetitively, as noted below. What are some aspects or phrases stated in the text associated with each word?

The Word
   v.1 (e.g., the Word was in the beginning)
   v.1_____
   v.1_____
   v.14_____

What similarities do you find between John 1:1 and Genesis 1:1? How might this appeal to a Jewish audience?

What does it mean for Jesus to be the Word? What in particular speaks to you in this?

Light
   v.4_____
   v.5_____
   v.7-8_____
   v.9_____

Based on the text, what does it mean for Jesus to be the light? What does it mean for Him to give light to every man?

How does the richness of this imagery add meaning to who Jesus is?

Life
v.4_____
v.4_____

What do you think it means for His life to be our light?

What does this verse mean to you personally?

The Greek word for *"life"* here is *zoe* which means so much more than mere physical life or eternal life, although it encompasses both. *Zoe* life means the fullness of life as God intended it to be, Holy Spirit given and Holy Spirit empowered through the saving work of Jesus Christ. It is fullness of life spiritually and physically, continuing into eternity. It gives life to our mind, will, and hearts as well. *Zoe* is used 36 times in the book of John.

Grace
v.14_____
v.16_____
v.17_____

John makes it clear to us that grace is one of the defining qualities of Jesus and, as the text also states, of God Himself. Is that a word you would use to describe Jesus? Why or why not?

Truth
v.14_____
v.17_____

Although we will study this more in the coming weeks, why do you think John used the word *"truth"* (along with *"grace"*) to describe Jesus?

Jesus came *"full of grace and truth"* and *"grace and truth came through Jesus."* What is the difference between these two statements?

2. In the middle of this packed and powerful introduction, John clearly states the way of salvation. Where is it in the text and what does it say?

This, then, is the tone John establishes for us in the introduction:

1) With great imagery and intent, he introduces us to Jesus, *God the Son,* who has come into the world.
2) He lays out the way of salvation, as he does throughout the book, because it is imperative to his message.
3) He gives us a foretaste of what will be revealed about Jesus in the coming pages: He *is* the light and life, and He *brings* light and life. This is a primary theme of the book. Darkness has not and will not overcome the light.
4) He reveals to us Jesus, who is *full* of grace and truth and *brings* grace and truth. Throughout the book of John, we will see grace and truth marking Jesus everywhere he moved.

Day 5

1. Read John 21:25. What is John saying here?

This is the only instance in the book of John where John steps out of third person narrative into the first person. Why do you think he does this? As we will soon see, John only shares a fraction of the many things Jesus did while walking on earth. Thus, the things he does write about are chosen very carefully and intentionally.

2. John makes very clear his intent and purpose in writing this gospel in John 20:31. What is it?

Again, John steps out of third person narrative, but this time into the second person, *"you,"* engaging the reader in a very direct way (the only time he does this in the entire book). Why do you think he does so?

Depending on the version of your Bible, you may see a notation that the phrase, *"that you might believe"* can also be translated to mean, *"may continue to believe."* How might this add depth to the meaning of the text? Also, the Greek word for *"life"* here is *zoe*. As mentioned earlier, this means much more than extending our life into eternity—it has enormous impact on the here and now. How might this add meaning to the text?

3. Read 2 Timothy 3:16-17. John is not the only author of this great book of the Bible. Who is the ultimate Author? What does this text say about Scripture?

As we open the book of John together in the coming weeks, my prayer is that in a very real way, you are saturated by the light and life of Jesus, and, as a result, increasingly grow as a person whose life and heart are intimately devoted to Christ.

Deepening our Devotion...

Each lesson will end with a more in depth look at someone in the text who encountered Jesus and experienced the loving light and life He offered them. Their devotion to Jesus—not merely to a creed or a religion—is a response to this great gift. They were ordinary people made extraordinary by Jesus.

A closer look at
John

"In Him was life, and that life was the light of men." John 1:4

Think about this for a moment. John was not a writer by trade, nor was he schooled in the religious circles of his time. Before meeting Jesus, he was just a fisherman. After that he was a disciple of Jesus for three years—sharing meals with Him, listening to His teaching, learning and shaping his life around Him. After Jesus' death and resurrection John, along with the other apostles, were the leaders of the early church. Clearly God inspired John to write this book of the Bible exactly as He wanted it, but He also used John just as he was—his personality, his relationship with Jesus, his writing style, etc.—to pen one of the most life-changing books ever written. I doubt John had any idea that his book would be read and treasured by millions, his words memorized by children (John 3:16) and studied by groups like yours 2,000 years later. John himself embodied the above verse: it was the life of Jesus in him that saturated his being and overflowed.

Although our influence may not be quite so dramatic, God uses ordinary people whose lives are surrendered to Him. Your life, my life. His life in us becomes the light that radiates in and through us.

*A Tale of Two Cities, by Charles Dickens
**The Hobbit, by J.R.R. Tolkien

Unveiling Jesus
Lesson 2
John 1:19–3:36

The focus of this week's lesson is twofold: 1) the great gift of *life* Christ offers both to us and to the people He puts in our path, and 2) the marvelous and revealing *light* of Jesus. But first, let us learn some from a man devoted to Jesus Christ—John the Baptist.

Day 1 *John the Baptist - John 1:19-34, 3:22-26*

1. Read John 1:19-28. According to this text, who is John the Baptist (not to be confused with John the disciple and author of this gospel) and why was his role so significant?

2. Read John 1: 29. What does John call Jesus?

This is the first public announcement of Jesus since the announcement of His birth. Why is this specific description important?

3. Read John 3:22-30. John the Baptist's entire purpose in life up to this point was to lead people to repentance and point them to the coming Messiah. Up until that day, people were following *him* as they waited for

the Messiah. Now that Jesus was here his role was shifting. What is John the Baptist saying in John 3:30? What do his words reveal about him?

Day 2 Jesus' First Miracle and the Clearing of the Temple – John 2

1. Read John 2:1-11. This was the first of eight miracles that Jesus performs in the book of John. It happened shortly after choosing his 12 disciples and took place in the small town of Cana with relatively few people around to witness it. What happened?

According to verse 11, what was the purpose of this miracle? Why was this important?

2. Read John 2:12-17. What was the issue here and why was Jesus troubled by it?

Do you think righteous anger has a place in a believer's life. If so, what?

What stirs you to righteous anger (e.g., injustice, manipulation of God's Word, etc)?

Days 3–4 Nicodemus and the Way to Eternal Life – John 3:1-18

1. Read John 3:1-3. What do we learn about Nicodemus from this text?

2. According to Jesus, *"unless a man is born again, he cannot see the kingdom of God"* (v.3). What do you think this means?

What role does the Spirit have in a person being born again (vs. 5-8)?

3. This text contains perhaps the most memorized verse of the Bible, John 3:16. It is simple enough for a child to understand and accept, yet profound enough that the wisest of men still weep upon hearing it. What does it say?

I do not know about you, but familiarity can make me dull to powerful truths. Let us try to freshen up this verse by looking at it a little more closely.

What drove God to send His Son into a lost and sinful world?

God gave Jesus to us. Nicodemus and others who heard and/or came to believe in Jesus up until the end of Jesus' earthly ministry likely had no idea the high price that would be paid for this gift. We, of course, know the great cost to Jesus and the Father. What was it?

"Whoever believes in him..." Jesus is the bridge from God and salvation to mankind, but we have a part in this as well. What is it?

"... will not perish." What does perish mean?

"...but have eternal life." What is the result of believing in Jesus? Keeping in mind our definition of *zoe* life as talked about last week, what is another way of saying *"eternal life"*?

4. Often people have an ungrounded notion that God is all about judgment and condemnation. How does John 3:17 address this?

a study on devotion to Jesus from the book of john

5. Using your own words, how would you explain John 3:16-17 to someone who is not a Christian?

6. This chapter isn't clear about Nicodemus' response to Jesus' offer of salvation, but we get the sense that he is puzzled about the concept of being born again. Nicodemus is mentioned two more times in John. What sense do you get of his spiritual progress in the following passages:

John 7:50-52

John 19:39-42

God works differently in every human heart. Sometimes a person comes to faith immediately upon hearing the truth of Jesus and the need to be spiritually born again; other times a person comes to faith and commitment over time. In the case of Nicodemus, the original hearer of John 3:16, we know initially that God awakened his heart (he approached Jesus with genuine spiritual interest), then, after several months we see him rather timidly defend Jesus to his fellow Pharisees, and finally after Jesus' death his actions boldly make a statement of allegiance. What encouragement do you get from this?

Everyone who is a follower of Jesus Christ has a story. For some of us it was a dramatic conversion; for others of us it was a slow and steady road to belief. What is your story of spiritual awakening and commitment to Jesus?

Day 5 *The Revealing Light of Christ – John 3:19-21*

1. Read John 3:19-21. What do you learn about the light of Christ in this text?

2. According to this text, what is one reason people will not come into the light? What does the light expose?

The reality is that some people will reject Christ not on intellectual grounds but on something more personal. What is it, according to this text?

3. *"Whoever lives by the truth comes into the light"* (v.21). What connection do you see between light and truth?

4. As we grow as believers in Christ, we grow more spiritually sensitive to things in our life that are not healthy for us or honoring to God. This is sanctification—the Holy Spirit shedding light on these areas of refining in our lives. Knowing Jesus is full of grace and truth, how should we respond to this kind of light? Those of us who *"live by the truth"* don't have to be afraid of letting God's light shine on us, even in our darkest places. Why?

Take some time and think about ways God has shown His loving light on your life. Perhaps He revealed a truth of Scripture to you, an insight into a blind spot in your life, or conviction of wrongdoing. Perhaps He enlightened you to see your gifts and talents or enabled you to forgive somebody. Record some of them here.

Deepening our Devotion...

A closer look at
John the Baptist

"He must become greater; I must become less."
John 3:30

It is often easy to recognize a person who grows to love attention and adulation more than the ministry they represent or the God who gave it to them. However, the temptation to grab the glory may be a little more subtle for the rest of us. When we are praised, respected, admired for our work in the kingdom of God—perhaps it is how we sing, how we teach, how we communicate, how we serve etc.—the question we need to keep before us is this: do we want people to see Jesus...or ourselves? John the Baptist squared off with this question and stated with conviction: He (Jesus) must become greater; I must become less.

The opposite, however, can be true as well. For some of us, we think we have nothing to offer so we linger in the depths when God wants to raise us up to touch another life or use our gifts for His purposes.

Take a moment to honestly examine your life in this area. Which way do you tend to gravitate: wanting self to stay in the limelight or letting insecurity keep God from using you or your gifts?

Depending on how you answered above, when are you most vulnerable to letting praise from people get to your head OR when are you most vulnerable to letting insecurity hold you back from being used by God?

Be encouraged! None of us do this perfectly, but as we grow in our relationship with Jesus and are saturated more and more with His light and life, a natural result for some of us will be a growing desire to have people see Jesus rather than ourselves, and for others it will be a growing confidence that we have much to offer the world.

I invite you right now to ask Jesus to shine his light of understanding on this area of your life that you might move forward in truth and confidence.

Encountering Christ
Lesson 3
John 4 and 5

Although Jesus undoubtedly encountered thousands of individuals during his earthly ministry, John carefully and intentionally chose a handful of these interactions to share in his gospel. This week's lesson focuses on Jesus' encounters with three very different people and the powerful effects of His touch on their life. Each encounter has a relevant message for each of us.

Day 1 Jesus' Encounter with the Samaritan Woman – John 4:1-42

John devotes almost an entire chapter to Jesus' encounter with the Samaritan woman, otherwise known as the woman at the well. A long history of tension and animosity existed between the Jews and the Samaritans. During Jesus' time, Jews disregarded Samaritans and actually spoke their name with contempt. Marriages between the two cultures were forbidden and social interactions were greatly restricted. Also, according to Jewish tradition, women were considered inferior during Jesus' time and men seldom spoke with them in public. In this context **read John 4:1-26.**

1. How did Jesus break tradition in this encounter?

2. What did Jesus offer her in v.10? What do you think He meant by this?

3. What do you think Jesus knew about her?

4. Look over this text again. What do you see in this encounter of the grace and truth of Jesus?

5. Did the woman have to get her act together before she could accept this great gift?

6. Why do you think John chose this story to share early on in his book?

Day 2 Jesus' Encounter with the Samaritan Woman - Part 2

1. Read John 4:27-42. After her encounter with Jesus, what did the Samaritan woman do?

2. According to v.39, why did many Samaritans from that town believe?

3. What is a testimony? How is it different from sharing the gospel?

4. The woman could have kept her encounter with Jesus to herself but instead, shared it. How can sharing our testimony make a difference?

5. Her testimony **pointed them to Jesus**. When they turned their attention to Jesus, what was the result (v.41)?

Our testimony does not save people; rather, our testimony turns other people to Jesus. Why is this so important for us to understand as we share our faith with others?

A testimony does not have to be a 30 minute presentation of our entire story; it can be a short snippet of something God has done in our lives. How does this truth lift some of the burden we may feel?

6. Sometimes we place so much burden on ourselves for other people's salvation. How does this story lift that burden?

Day 3 Jesus' Encounter with the Royal Official – John 4:43-54

1. This story is the first miracle of healing recorded in the book of John. It is a brief encounter, at least as it is recorded, but is included for a reason, as we will soon see. Read John 4:43-54. What strikes you in this passage?

2. We know from John 2:23 and John 4:45 that Jesus had performed many other miraculous signs, but it appears that He was present during them. When the official approached Jesus, he asked Jesus to come with him to heal his child. How did Jesus respond and how did this stretch the official's faith?

a study on devotion to Jesus from the book of john

3. What is the key phrase in v.50 that we can apply to our lives?

4. Do you think that there are points in our lives where we can choose to either take Jesus at His word or not take Him at His word? What might these look like? Can you think of a time when you chose to take Jesus at His word?

5. This text also encourages us to come to Jesus on behalf of other people, particularly our children. Is there a need out there that you can bring to Jesus on behalf of someone else? Take a moment to do so now.

Days 4–5 Jesus' Encounter with the Paralytic – John 5

1. Read John 5:1-16. The exchange recorded here between Jesus and the man is relatively brief. Note the exchange below:

Jesus v.6:_____
Paralytic v.7:_____
Jesus v.8:_____

Does anything strike you about this exchange?

Who initiated this exchange? How might that be relevant?

If Jesus asked you today, "Do you want to get well?," would that question resonate in your heart? How would you respond? If it is relevant to you now, take a moment to talk to Him about it.

2. Where did the true power of healing lie?

3. What day of the week did this happen?

4. One would think that people would rejoice over the healing and be happy for the man. Instead, what happened?

The Sabbath was given by God to His people for their good (Luke 2:27); it was a day designated by God to cease from work and to rest. However, the Pharisees of the time turned the Sabbath into something it was never meant to be, adding thousands of detailed rules and definitions of "work" (e.g., it was unlawful to move furniture on the Sabbath—there was an exception to this: you could move a ladder, but only four steps). Somewhere the line became blurred as to what was God's law and what was man-made law. Jesus never broke God's law; He did, however, break those rules made by man. There are several instances throughout all four gospels where Jesus healed or did something controversial on the Sabbath.

5. Clearly, God wants us to obey and follow His commands. Sometimes even for us, however, the line gets blurred between God's commands and man-made rules. Can you think of an example in the Christian church where this is the case?

7. As you think about these three individuals that encountered Jesus, what conclusions can you draw about the types of people Jesus reached?

8. John 5:17-47 records Jesus' response to the Jews who were furious with His healing on the Sabbath. The content is rich in this text but for now we will focus on two points Jesus makes.

Read John 5:39-40. What do you think Jesus is saying here?

When we study the Scriptures, our study should not merely be an intellectual pursuit (although it certainly is that), but it should always move us to Christ. Jesus Himself gives life to the words. The Jews Jesus spoke to in this text diligently studied the Scriptures because they thought *"that by them they might possess eternal life"* and yet they failed to see the Son of God standing in their midst! How might we do that very thing as we study the Scriptures?

Read John 5:44. What is Jesus saying here and what can we, as followers of Jesus Christ, learn from it?

Seeking the praise of other people can often win out over seeking praise from God. We all struggle with it to varying degrees, but Jesus wants our words, actions, and motives be first and foremost to please Him. Take a moment to examine yourself in this area and write any thoughts you have below.

Deepening our Devotion...

A closer look at
The Woman at the Well

"He told me everything I ever did."
John 4:39

What captured this woman's heart wasn't just the living water Jesus offered her and the glorious revelation that He was the Messiah. These were certainly the components of a life changing encounter. What captured her was that Jesus knew her story. Jesus said to her, "The fact is, you have had five husbands, and the man you now have is not your husband." Think about how many stories are behind that statement. He knew where there was sin, but He also knew where there was sorrow, fear, pain, and so many other things. He knew the stories behind the story—*everything* that brought her to this moment in time. And, accompanying this knowledge was conviction…forgiveness… acceptance… healing…unconditional love. There were no more secrets, no more shame, no more feeling misunderstood. Jesus had shown the light of grace and truth on her life and she was now set free. A new story was about to begin.

Our devotion to Jesus deepens as we live in the truth that He knows us, knows our story, and knows the story behind the story. He knows our motives (good and bad), knows our weaknesses and frailties, knows where we are vulnerable to making bad choices and that which enables us to make good ones; knows when we have been hurt by another and when we have hurt someone else. He knows the truth of it all even better than we do. Not only does He know, but He wants to bring life-giving water into every area. This is living in *zoe* life, paved by His grace and truth. The freedom this brings is priceless. Take some time and think about your story. Have you let His light shine into every area of it? Do you move with increased freedom because Jesus' life has saturated it? I invite you to surrender your story completely to Him.

a study on devotion to Jesus from the book of john

Food for Life
Lesson 4
John 6 and 7

This week's lesson speaks clearly and directly to the life Jesus offers. Though He offers life to all, many of His followers at the time begin to fall away, claiming that Jesus' teachings are too hard. Amidst this, however, we see that the disciples' allegiance to Jesus is strengthened, inspiring those of us who follow Christ some 2,000 years later.

Days 1–2 *Jesus Performs Miracles – John 6:1-24*

The events recorded in Chapter 6 occur over two days. In this text we see two of the eight miracles recorded in the book of John.

1. Read John 6:1-15. It is interesting to note that this miracle is the only miracle Jesus performed that is included in all four gospels. What was the actual miracle that took place?

2. There is so much in this text worth exploring, but our emphasis here will be on those who were engaged in the unfolding of this miracle. Jesus could have chosen to feed all these people any way He wanted, but He chose to involve a boy and a group of men.

The Boy
According to John 6:8-9 what is presented to Jesus?

What did Jesus do with it, according to 6:10-11? How much did the people get?

The text does not explicitly say that the boy initiated the exchange by coming forward with his small offering, but we can safely infer that he was willing to share what he had. What can we learn from this?

If I were that boy, I wonder if I would have protectively held on to my small portion of food—either out of selfishness or common sense—knowing that what I had was enough only for a couple of people. By being willing to share, the boy and the people experienced great blessing. Though the text does not tell us, how do think this could have impacted this boy's life?

Is there anything that is "yours" that you might offer to Jesus, knowing that he can take what little we offer and multiply it? Perhaps it is as mundane as your time today or as significant as a sacrificial financial gift. Take some time right now to ponder this and offer back to God whatever it is that He might be prompting in you.

The Disciples

How did Jesus involve the disciples in this miracle? How do you think that impacted them?

God often allows us to be a part of His blessing on other people. He might prompt us to say something, do something, intercede in prayer—any number of things. Have you ever experienced the joy of letting God use you to do a work in someone else's life? Take a moment to share about it.

3. Read John 6:16-21. What was the miracle that took place?

How was this different from other miracles?

Why do you think it was important enough for John to include here?

Day 3 *Jesus Teaches the Crowd – John 6: 25-71*

John 6:25-71. The Setting: Jesus had fed the 5,000 the day before but had withdrawn from the crowds because the people had wanted to make Him their king. He is now on the other side of the lake with His disciples, where the people once again have met Him. His focus now is to teach them about food that endures to eternal life.

The Teaching

1. Read John 6: 25-59, noting below references to *"bread"* and *"life."*

2. Let us direct our focus to some key truths in Jesus' teaching:

John 6:29   Doing good works alone does not give us life and salvation, but there is one work that we must do. What is it?

John 6:35   What does it mean that those who eat of Him will never hunger again?

John 6:40   What is the Father's will?

3. How would you summarize what Jesus means when He says He is the bread of life?

The Response

4. Read John 6:60-71. We begin to see more and more in the book of John that Jesus' teachings and actions lead to decision-making moments for those who hear. According to the following verses, how did the *"disciples"* (which included all who were following him at the time, not just the twelve) respond to Jesus' teaching?

John 6:60

John 6:66

I had a friend who could not get past the fact that God mandated animal sacrifice in the Old Testament. She found it highly offensive and told me she could not follow a God who would do such a thing. People—then and now—often make life-changing decisions based on a lack of understanding or misunderstanding of God and his Word. Others rationalize that Jesus' expectations are too hard, either intellectually or morally. This is what happened to some of Jesus' followers in the above verses. Some could not get beyond the literal to see the spiritual metaphor; others found the cost of following Jesus too high.

5. Now read Peter's powerful response in John 6:67-69. How does this contrast with the above responses?

6. What do you do when faced with a teaching of Jesus that is either hard to believe, disagreeable, or difficult to understand? What encouragement or challenge do you get from Peter's response?

a study on devotion to Jesus from the book of john

Day 4 *Teaching the People - John 7, 8:12*

The events and teaching that occur in chapter 7-9 appear to take place during and immediately following the Feast of Tabernacles. In Chapter 7—the focus of the rest of this week's lesson—Jesus boldly proclaims His presence as the living water and the light of the world. A little bit of background on the Feast of Tabernacles will help give insight into the magnitude of Jesus' claims.

The Feast of Tabernacles took place in Jerusalem during September/October and lasted eight days. It was a joyful celebration declared by God to commemorate God's deliverance of His people out of Egypt and His provision for them as they wandered in the desert for 40 years. It was also a joyful celebration of God's current and continued provision for His people and was one of eight feasts decreed by God.* More pertinent to our study, however, are the two very symbolic elements that took place during the celebration: the symbol of life giving water and the symbol of light. Understanding these provides valuable context to Jesus' teaching.

Jesus and the symbol of life-giving water

On the last day of the Feast of Tabernacles—known as the "Great Day"—a sacrificial pouring out of water (called a "water libation") was performed at the Temple. During the ceremony, the high priest would lead a procession of worshippers and flute players to the Pool of Siloam, where he would fill a golden pitcher of water and then return to the courtyard of the temple. The high priest then poured out the water on the alter while the people chanted parts of Psalm 118 with great joy. The ceremony was to thank God for His provision and pray for rain for the crops in the coming year. It also held prophetic significance, symbolizing that one day the knowledge of the Lord will cover the earth as the waters cover the sea.** Now, as you **read John 7:37-44**, picture Jesus at the temple on the last "Great Day" of the feast, saying these words. What was Jesus' bold statement and invitation?

In light of the above context, how does Jesus' invitation in vs. 37-38 hold special meaning? What is He saying?

Jesus and the symbol of light

At the end of the first day of the Feast of Tabernacles, four giant candelabras (each about 75 feet tall) were lit in the temple court while Levitical musicians played instruments in joyful celebration to the Lord. With the temple being on a hill, the whole city could see their glorious display. The light was to remind the people how God's Shekinah glory once filled the temple.*** Now, picture Jesus, standing in the temple court a day after the Feast, as you **read John 8:12.** What is the significance of His statement?

Day 5 The Response of the People - John 7:40-5

Once again in Chapter 7 we see a similar progress as in Chapter 6: Jesus teaches and the people are divided in their response. However, between Jesus' teaching and the *"people of Jerusalem's"* response, John allows us to witness some of the dialogue that leads to their decision making. Read John 7:40-52.

1. What is the common argument in the following verses:

John 7: 27, 41-43, 52

What does Isaiah 9:1-7 say about this?

What can you conclude about their reasoning?

2. Some people in this text made life-changing decisions not to believe in Jesus because of an incomplete or inaccurate understanding of Scripture. Do you see this in today's culture? If so, how?

3. And so, once again, the response of the people is divided. Some hate Jesus and try to seize him (v.30), yet many put their faith in him (v.31).

a study on devotion to Jesus from the book of john

What do you observe about the guards who were sent to arrest Jesus (vs.45-46) and how do the chief priests respond to them? How about Nicodemus?

4. Have you ever experienced something similar to what the guards and Nicodemus experienced when standing up for Christ?

Deepening our Devotion...

A closer look at **Peter**

"You do not want to leave too, do you?," Jesus asked the Twelve. Simon Peter answered him, "Lord to whom shall we go? You have the words of eternal life." John 6:67-68

Peter and the disciples were surrounded by others who were also struggling to understand Jesus' teaching. Some were followers of Jesus; others were skeptical Jews. Many fell away at this point because either their minds or their wills could not accept Jesus' teaching—it was "hard" (v.60) or it was "offensive" (v.61).

As we grow in our relationship with Christ we can handle the harder teachings before us. Certainly we may not understand them or we may struggle with surrendering to them, but our trust in Jesus and who He is increasingly trumps our lack of understanding. This is evidence of spiritual growth—we claim our allegiance to Him because we know He is God and is completely trustworthy and good. The disciples likely did not fully understand all Jesus' teaching in His discourse on being the bread of life (we see many times in the Bible where they didn't understand what Jesus was trying to teach them), but their trust in Jesus held their allegiance.

Just like the disciples, deepened devotion to Jesus is *demonstrated and developed* by decisions to trust in times of difficulty, but it is also *cultivated* in our daily life of living in relationship with Him.

Are you in a situation now where you are struggling whether or not to trust Jesus with something—maybe it is something in the Bible or something in your circumstances you do not understand? Go to Him, trust Him. Make a conscious choice to say, "Jesus, I don't understand this, but I believe YOU and who You are. Lord, to whom else shall I go? You alone have the words of eternal life." He alone has the words to true and eternal *zoe* life. Surrender your uncertainty to His sovereignty.

*"The Festival of Sukkot: the Feast of Tabernacles," Hebrew for Christians (www.hebrew4christinas.com)

**"The Feast of Tabernacles" by Day of Discovery.

***"Finding Jesus in the Feast of Tabernacles," Christian Broadcasting Network (www.cbn.com)

a study on devotion to Jesus from the book of john

Called to Live in Light
Lesson 5
John 8–9

As was mentioned in last week's lesson, it appears that John 7-9 takes place during or immediately following the eight day Feast of Tabernacles in Jerusalem. This week's lesson continues with Jesus' movement and teaching around the temple and in Jerusalem, concluding with a very pertinent and beautiful story of healing.

Day 1 *Jesus' Encounter with the Adulterous Woman - John 8:1-11*

You will likely find a notation in your Bible that many of the earliest and most reliable manuscripts do not include this text. Indeed, this text breaks stylistically from the flow of John 7 and 8, which makes it somewhat of a mystery. However, most scholars agree that it is historically authentic and should remain in the gospel of John.* In this study, we will treat it in chronological progression in chapters 7 and 8.

The Setting: This captivating story of Jesus' encounter with the woman caught in adultery takes place in the temple courts as Jesus is teaching the people. The day before was the *"last and greatest day of the Feast"* in which Jesus proclaimed to the people that He alone satisfied the thirst of individuals and offered living water to those who believed in Him. This encounter takes place right before Jesus proclaims Himself the light of the world (see last week's notes on the symbolic significance of living water and light during the Feast of Tabernacles). Because it so beautifully captures the grace of Jesus, we will spend the first day of this week's lesson on it.

1. Read John 8:1-11. Old Testament law required that someone caught in adultery be stoned. Jesus, however, offers her something else. What did He offer her and how does this demonstrate the heart of Christ?

2. Does this story imply that we are to disregard sin? Why or why not?

3. What two or three lessons do you take away from this text based on Jesus' words and actions?

4. Can you think of a time when you experienced someone's grace when you really deserved judgment? How did it feel?

Day 2 *Jesus Teaches the People – John 8:12-58*

If you recall from last week's lesson, Jesus' proclaimed in John 8:12 that He was the light of the world. This bold proclamation triggered the teaching and dialogue with the Jews that follows. Although there is much to explore here, we will limit our focus to a couple key points of Jesus' teaching.

1. Throughout this chapter, we see many allusions to the unity between Jesus and the Father. Jot some of these below.

In fact, throughout the entire book of John, we see dozens of verses that speak to this unity. Why do you think this is important?

a study on devotion to Jesus from the book of john

2. Jesus repeatedly offers His listeners the way of salvation throughout the entire book of John. Where do you see it in chapter 8?

3. After much heated dialogue between Jesus and the Jews, John ends this section with a profound statement from Jesus in v.58. What is it?

Read Exodus 3:13-14. The Jews in Jesus' time clearly understood what "I AM" meant. What insight does the text in Exodus 3 give you?

What is Jesus saying here?

Why did the Jews react so violently?

Days 3—5 *The Healing of a Man Born Blind - John 9*

Remember, John is strategic and intentional in the writing of his book, as is Jesus in the way He moved and taught. It appears that Jesus' encounter with this man occurred the same day as His great "I am!" statement at the end of Chapter 8. What we know for certain is that it is the Sabbath and that Jesus is in Jerusalem. John devotes an entire chapter to this story; indeed, it is a story very much worth our time and attention.

The Healing John 9:1-7

1. State the facts of the healing below.

2. According to verse 3, why was this man born blind? What insight does this give you about the possible purpose of trials we go through?

What do you think was the *"work of God"* displayed in his life that Jesus was alluding to?

3. What reference to *"light"* is given here and what does Jesus mean by it?

4. According to vs. 6-7, two actions were performed that were part of the healing process, one by Jesus and one by the blind man. What were they and why do you think Jesus healed in this manner?

What was the choice the blind man had to make?

What insight do you gain from this text about the value of obedience? If you have a moment, read 2 Kings 5:1-14 to gain further insight on this.

Can you identify a time in your life where you have reaped the benefit of obeying God (e.g., a command in Scripture, a prompting of the Holy Spirit, a call to trust)? Share below.

What do you remember about the Pool of Siloam from last week's lesson? Do you think the reference here is coincidental?

a study on devotion to Jesus from the book of john

The Response to the Healing John 9:8-34

1. Once again, we see that the Pharisees are not happy about the wonderful work of God demonstrated in this man's life. What are they concerned about?

2. John 9:22 tells us that there was a severe penalty for anyone who believed Jesus was the Messiah. What was it?

This penalty meant forever exclusion from worship at the synagogue as well as exclusion from fellowship and interaction with people.** In light of this, and from the dialogue with the Pharisees, what do you see of the man's courage and fortitude in this text?

The Pharisees respond quite emotionally to the man's statements. How do they respond according to vs. 28 and 34?

Even back in Jesus' time, there was a high cost to standing up for Jesus—persecution, insults, excommunication, hatred. Do you see this in today's American culture? How about in other places in the world?

Finally, what happens to the man in verse 34?

The Follow Up Encounter with Jesus John 9:35-41

1. Read John 9:35-41. What beautiful aspect of Jesus do you see in v.35: *"Jesus heard that they had thrown him out, and when He (Jesus) found him...."*?

What encouragement can we find in this?

In John 9:35-38 we see a powerful and complete transformation in this man as Jesus fully reveals Himself. Suddenly everything is clear; he is no longer physically blind, nor is he spiritually blind. At the beginning of this story Jesus says that this man was born blind so that the *"work of God might be displayed in his life."* Which do you think was the greater work of God in his life, gaining physical sight or gaining spiritual sight?

Sometimes we narrow our understanding of miracles to include only those in the physical realm, when actually miracles might be occurring in such things as emotional healing, spiritual awakening, being used by God, etc. What are some ways the work of God has been displayed in your life?

Although the Bible does not tell us, my guess is that this man would go through all his years of suffering again to gain this great spiritual blessing. Has God ever used a hardship in your life to bring about spiritual growth?

2. As you consider the entire story of the healing, persecution, and salvation of the man born blind, what speaks to you personally?

Deepening our Devotion...

A closer look at
The Man Born Blind

"Go," Jesus told him, "wash in the pool of Siloam"(this word means Sent). So the man went and washed, and came home seeing."
John 9:7

It is not unusual throughout the Bible for a *"work of God to be displayed"* in someone's life, the recipient has to obey something the Lord has commanded. Maybe it is hard or maybe it doesn't make sense, but the call is to obey, regardless. The man born blind had a choice before him: was he going to obey Jesus' command to wash in the pool of Siloam or not? The command was not for Jesus' sake—He certainly didn't need the pool for the healing to happen. The command was for the man's sake. The direction his life would take hinged on that choice. And, so, for a spiritual moment time stood still.

God often works similarly in our lives, commanding we obey something before He moves. Why do you think God works this way?

Sometimes the choice to obey is easy or obvious; other times it is hard or costly. The call to obey takes all kinds of forms: a clear command of Scripture, a prompting of the Spirit, a prick in our conscience. And the voices that try to keep us from obeying? Believe me, I know them all: pride, fear, logic, laziness, doubt, insecurity, etc. Increased obedience, however, is the evidence of growth in our spiritual lives and devotion to Jesus Christ. Obedience demonstrates our trust in Jesus and opens doors for places God wants to take us. Obeying God is our call—*and it is our blessing*. "Even the smallest bit of obedience opens heaven, and the deepest truths of God immediately become ours." (Oswald Chambers)

*The Gospel of John, by Herman Ridderbos, p. 287
**Barnes' Notes on the Book of John, Albert Barnes.

Saturated in the Light and Life of Christ

Called to Live in Life
Lesson 6
John 10–11

If you will recall last week's lesson, John devoted a significant amount of time (all of Chapter 9) to the story of God's working in the life of the man born blind. A majority of this week's lesson will focus on the story of Lazarus (Chapter 11). Although we know from the end of Chapter 10 that some time had elapsed between the two miracles, we also know that word of the blind man's healing had spread and was known by those who witnessed Lazarus' resurrection from the dead (John 11:37). Between these two dramatic, well chosen stories—light out of darkness and life out of death—is Jesus' teaching on shepherd and sheep.

Day 1 A Shepherd and His Sheep – John 10

1. As you read this chapter, make note of the references to shepherd and sheep below:

<u>Shepherd</u>
e.g. v2 enters by the gate

<u>Sheep</u>
v3 listen to his voice

2. Jesus offers these precious shepherd/sheep truths of John 10 to those listening at the time and the millions of readers thereafter. What are three or four significant implications for you as a follower of Jesus Christ?

3. What kind of life does your Shepherd offer you (v.10)? Once again, the word for *"life"* here is *zoe*. What do you think this *zoe* life means in real day to day living for a believer in Jesus Christ?

Days 2–5   *The Story of Lazarus – John 11*

1. Read John 11:1-16.

Who is Lazarus and what kind of relationship did he and his sisters have with Jesus?

Let us take a moment and note the unfolding of events here. How is each described:

    Mary alerts Jesus to the situation v.3

    Jesus declares what will happen v.4

    Jesus' decides what they will do v.6

We have the benefit of knowing what happens at the end of this story, but Mary, Martha, Lazarus, and the disciples did not. What do you think Mary and Martha felt when Jesus didn't come during those four days and Lazarus died? What would you have felt?

What have you thought and felt when God has been silent in your life and circumstances?

Why do you think Jesus waited two more days before leaving to see Lazarus?

2. Read John 11:17-44.

"On his arrival, Jesus found that Lazarus had already been in the tomb for four days." On first appearances, it seems that Jesus is too late. However, God's timing is always perfect. How was it perfect in this story?

Could Jesus have healed Lazarus before he died? Of course. He certainly had done that with other people. Why do you think He chose to raise Lazarus from the dead rather than heal him and how did it fulfill His statement in John 11:4b?

Read John 11:33, 35, 38. What do you see of Jesus in these verses?

Even though Jesus knew what He was going to do, He was still deeply moved and wept over their grief. Why do you think this is?

a study on devotion to Jesus from the book of john

Jesus is a tender friend who cares deeply about us. We can come to Him with our grief or our broken heart knowing that He is compassionate and tenderhearted. Is there something breaking your heart right now? He knows and, yes, He cares deeply.

Not only does Jesus care deeply, He has the power to move with a word and do what is seemingly impossible. What does He say and do, according to John 11:43-44?

As you look at this story in its entirety up to verse 44, how do you think Mary and Martha's understanding of and faith in Jesus grew?

3. Read John 11:45-46. What are the two very different responses to Jesus raising Lazarus from the dead?

Does this sound familiar from other passages we have looked at? Do you think John is communicating a general truth about the different ways people respond to Jesus? If so, what is that insight?

4. Read John 11:47-57. We see throughout the book of John that people often reject Jesus with strong emotion, often defying rationality. Why do you think this is?

As we see in many other places in John, the movement of God quite often leads to a decision-making moment. What did the Sanhedrin decide at this time?

5. Read John 12:9-11.

What did the chief priests decide to do to Lazarus and why?

As we see in this story and in the story of the man born blind, when the work of God is displayed in our life (in any number of ways, not just physical healing), it may come with a cost. For Lazarus, it was being put on a hit list; for the man born blind, it was ridicule and being cast out of the synagogue. With both of these men, the blessings far outweighed the cost and their allegiance to Jesus was firm. Are you inspired and/or encouraged by these stories? If so, how?

6. On the other hand, many people came to faith in Christ because of the work of God in both the man born blind and in Lazarus' life. Often God's working in our life is for a greater purpose than just our benefit. Take a moment or two to think about a time where others benefitted from God's movement in your life. Share below.

7. The stories told by John in Chapters 9 and 11 have many similarities and some differences. The themes of light and life are clearly demonstrated by Jesus in these texts. Here are some of them:

The Healing of the Man Born Blind	The Raising of Lazarus
1. Jesus brought light from darkness	1. Jesus brought life from death
2. Before miracle Jesus said: "...this (blindness) happened so the work of God might be displayed in his life." 9:3	2. Before miracle Jesus said: "this (sickness) is for God's glory so that God's Son may glorified through it." 11:4
3. Before miracle Jesus referred himself as: "I am the light of the world." 9:5	3. Before miracle Jesus referred to to himself as: "I am the resurrection and the life." 11:25
4. Pharisees objected	4. Pharisees objected
5. The man was persecuted	5. Lazarus was persecuted
6. Word of his healing spread	6. Word of his resurrection spread and many came to faith in Christ
7. The man participated in the miracle by obeying Jesus' command	7. Jesus called Lazarus back to life
8. This man was a stranger	8. Lazarus was a friend of Jesus
9. Jesus initiated the encounter	9. Lazarus' sisters initiated the encounter
10. Other?	

Are there any themes or lessons we can draw from the above?

9. Do you see any connection between the teachings on the shepherd and his sheep and these two stories? If so, what?

Deepening our Devotion...

A closer look at **Mary, Martha, and sheep**

"...and the sheep follow Him because they know His voice." John 10:4

As we look closely at the story of Lazarus, it doesn't take long to see that so much more is going on than restoring physical life to a man dead for four days. This a story that powerfully offers insight into how Jesus moves in the lives of those who belong to Him. Yes, Mary, Martha and Lazarus experienced it, but it is also very pertinent to your life and my life as well.

In this story we see that:
~Jesus' plans, purposes and how He accomplishes them are usually far different and far better than we plan, expect, or even hope for.
~Jesus has compassion for us and what we are going through, but also the power to do something about it. Both are part of who He is and how He moves.
~Jesus often has a bigger picture of purpose and blessing than what He is doing in the immediate situation.

Often God's silence in our circumstances can lead us to draw conclusions that are inaccurate, e.g., God doesn't care, He doesn't realize the urgency of the situation, He isn't really in control, He doesn't really want to help, etc. Is there something going on in your life where it seems God is silent? Are you tempted to draw conclusions like those listed above?

Can you think of a situation in your past when you felt God's silence when you were in a place of need, yet realized later that He was in control all along?

The more we understand and experience God's sovereign control and His desire to do more than all we ask or imagine, the more we long to follow no other voice but His, for this is the voice we trust.

a study on devotion to Jesus from the book of john

Devotion Poured Out
Lesson 7
John 12–13

This week's lesson will focus on two events, both of which demonstrate radical, extravagant, and sacrificial love. There are many parallels in these beautiful texts, yet they uniquely capture different aspects of our relationship with Jesus.

Day 1 Mary's Extravagant Love – John 12:1-8

It is one week before Jesus' death. It is not clear whose house the story takes place, but we do know the dinner is given in Jesus' honor and Mary, Martha, and Lazarus are there with Jesus, along with the disciples.

1. What do you know about Mary from last week's lesson and the other gospels (e.g., Luke 10:38-42)?

2. What did Mary do in this text?

3. Do you think it had the perception of being scandalous? Wasteful?

4. Although it may have raised a few eyebrows in the room, what do you think drove Mary to do what she did? How does Jesus respond?

5. How do Jesus' words in John 7:24 apply here?

6. Have you ever set practicality aside and lavished on someone you love? What drove you? What did it communicate? How was it received?

7. Indeed, if the perfume had been sold, it would have helped many poor people. Does this mean Jesus doesn't care for the poor? Obviously not. However, there is a time and place for extravagant, sacrificial and demonstrative love for Jesus in our lives. What might be some examples nowadays? How about for you?

8. It is unlikely that Mary realized Jesus would die in a few days and yet Jesus says, *"It was meant that she should save this perfume for the day of my burial."* How might this demonstrate how God can take our acts of devotion and use them for greater purposes than what we realize at the time?

Day 2 *John 12:42-46*

1. Fear can be a debilitating power in a person's life. How do we see it in these people's lives?

2. Do you think fear and its effects need to rule us? What can have power over it?

3. How might we demonstrate that we love praise from men more than praise from God?

4. What does Jesus say about light and darkness in verse 46?

5. How might this tie in with living in fear?

Days 3–4 Jesus' Extravagant Love – John 13:1-17

It is significant to note that one third of the book of John is devoted to the last few hours of Jesus' life. For three years, Jesus has been in public ministry, all the while teaching and training His disciples. Now, as we see in chapters 13-17, Jesus directs all of his attention to these 11 men (for Judas would betray Him shortly) whom He loves deeply and who will spread His light and love, His grace and truth. What Jesus communicates now matters. And so, with great intentionality, love, and foresight, Jesus speaks—through word and action—and profoundly ministers to His disciples. This was not only for them, however, it is for us who follow Him as well. As we focus on Jesus' teaching over the next 2 ½ lessons, we too will discover the heartbeat of discipleship.

Read John 13:1-17

1. Knowing a little bit about sandals, feet, and the culture at the time, how do Jesus actions demonstrate humility?

2. As you initially read this text, what do you think Jesus was communicating to His disciples?

What insight do the following verses give to this:

v.1b

v.8b

v.14b-15

v.16

v.34

3. As any good teacher knows, there are times when teaching is most effective when an action is involved rather than words alone. How were Jesus' actions here more effective than mere words?

4. Do you think the disciples were surprised by what Jesus was doing? Why?

5. According to verse 17, there is a difference between knowing something and doing something. When are we blessed and what do you think that blessing looks like?

6. What parallels do you see in Mary and Jesus' acts of love?

Day 5 A Closer Look at Peter

Read John 13:6-9

There is something refreshing about Peter. Perhaps it is his zeal or perhaps his authenticity. Peter lays it out there: the good, the bad, and the ugly. Let us take a moment to look at his exchange with Jesus in the midst of the feet washing. There is much to learn here.

Peter v.6: *"Lord, are you going to wash my feet?"*
Jesus v.7: *"You do not realize now what I am doing, but later you will understand."*
Peter v.8: *"No, you shall never wash my feet."*
Jesus v.8: *"Unless I wash you, you have no part with me."*
Peter v.9: *"Then, Lord, not just my feet but my hands and my head as well!"*

1. Peter knew Jesus was God. It was out of humility and sincere reverence for Jesus that he verbally spoke what the others were perhaps thinking: "How can I possibly let *You*, Jesus the Son of God, wash *my* feet? The mere thought is crazy!" Have you ever been surprised by something God has shown you about Himself? Perhaps it is a new understanding about His character, how He moves, or what is important to Him?

Do you think you might have any preconceived ideas about God that might be incomplete or inaccurate, and, more importantly, are you open to let Him reveal more of Himself to you?

2. I wonder how many times in my life God has thought, *"You do not realize now what I am doing, but later you will understand."* There are many, many things that happen in our lives that we do not understand at the time. Someday, though, we will. In that in-between time God wants us to have a heart and a will that surrenders in trust. Is God doing something in your life right now that you do not understand? Take a moment now to talk to Him about it and, if possible, yield it to Him.

3. Follow Peter here. Jesus explains that He needs to wash Peter's feet, but Peter still refuses. Yes, it seems his motives are sincere, but he needs to let Jesus teach him. Jesus then firmly corrects him. How does Peter respond? What do you think is going on in Peter's mind and heart?

4. What might Peter have missed out on if he had persisted in not allowing Jesus to wash his feet?

5. We see something similar in Acts 10 when God gives Peter a startling dream in which He instructs him three times to eat food which was clearly considered impure or defiled for the Jews. The dream is perplexing, for it goes against Peter's sound understanding of God and His ways. Later the dream would be interpreted to reveal God's plan to bring the gospel message to the Gentiles, a concept shocking to everyone, Jews and Gentiles alike. If you have a moment, read Acts 10:1-11:18. How do you think Peter's experience in John 13 prepared him for this?

Read John 13:31-38

6. From what you know of Peter and his personality, do you think he was sincere when he said to Jesus in v.37, *"I will lay down my life for you."*?

7. Of course, we know what happens in John 18:17, 25, and 27—Peter denies Jesus three times as Jesus predicted. Self-reliance, however well intentioned it may be, is not enough to live the Christian life. Reliance on ourselves will often leave us frustrated, ineffective, or, like Peter, in failure. We just are not enough, in and of ourselves. We may have a charismatic presence, a winsome personality, or courage of steel, but we are flawed and fallible people. One key element in our growth as followers of Jesus Christ is an increased understanding that we need Jesus and His strength in every area of our life. The growing Christian grows in dependence on Him. Can you think of examples in your life where this is true?

8. John does not leave us with Peter's failure, for failure is often a means for growth. In John 21:15-17, Jesus beautifully reaffirms Peter. What do you think is going on in this conversation? How do you think this impacted Peter and his future ministry?

9. As we live out our Christian life, there will be times when we fail—either in small moments or big. What do you learn personally from this text about failure, forgiveness, and reaffirmation?

Deepening our Devotion...

A closer look at **Mary**

"Then Mary took about a pint of pure nard, an expensive perfume; she poured it on Jesus feet and wiped it with her hair." John 12:3

Mary's extravagant act was a tangible demonstration of a heart overflowing with love, gratitude, and devotion to Jesus—a heart that *could not help* but pour out to her Lord. We don't really know if it was planned or spontaneous, but what we do see is that she gave Jesus her best at that moment in time and in the best way she knew how. The cost? Whether it was financial (the perfume was worth a lot of money) or personal (she would very likely be misunderstood or criticized)—the cost didn't really matter.

Have you ever been in a similar situation where you could not help but overflow with love or gratitude? Perhaps it was raising your hands in worship, writing a sacrificial check for the cause of Christ, or giving Him you life in the quiet of your heart. How it looks is different for each one of us at different moments in time, but it has this in common: it overflows from a full heart, it cares little about what other people think, and it sacrifices something to do so. There is a time and place to demonstrate this kind of devotion to Jesus. Embrace those moments when they come.

Take some time to think about your own unique ways that you can give your best to Jesus—your money, your time, your talents…even your very heart.

The Heart of Devoted Discipleship
Lessons 8–9
John 14, 15, 16, 17

It is the last few hours before His arrest and Jesus is sharing a quiet Passover meal with his disciples. Jesus knows His death is imminent and is spending this precious time with these men. He has just washed His disciples' feet, Judas has left to betray Him, and now Jesus is continuing to impart precious truths to the eleven. John—the writer of this gospel—is present, absorbing it all. If there is anything Jesus clearly wants His disciples to know, now is His time to say it. We would be wise to listen carefully to Jesus' words here. Indeed, John 14-17 provide truths that make up the heartbeat of the life of a disciple devoted to Jesus Christ, both then and now. Because this is a lengthy discussion between Jesus and His disciples and is meant to be heard as a whole, we will combine this section to include lessons 8 and 9.

The heart of discipleship is all about a relationship with Jesus. It is this relationship with Jesus that will sustain, nurture, and bring vibrancy and purpose to our existence. It is this relationship that will equip, empower, and multiply our ministry to the people and world around us. Because of this significance, our entire focus here will be on Jesus' teachings on this relationship.

Read John 14:1-16:33 in one sitting before answering the following questions. As you read this, picture the 11 disciples sitting quietly, listening to Jesus. Realize, though, that He is speaking to you, for in His

a study on devotion to Jesus from the book of john

foreknowledge He knew His words would one day be put into a book of the Bible that would reach the hands and hearts of millions of individuals, including you.

Days 1—3   *Jesus: the Way, the Truth, the Life – John 14:1-7*

We will begin with this short text. These verses form a small section of a much longer discourse, but are very worthy of our time and attention.

As disciples of Jesus Christ, it is important that we have a sound theology and understanding of salvation—both for ourselves and for others as we share Christ. Equally important, however, is the need to have a living active faith and relationship with Jesus that affects every aspect of our lives. This passage addresses both our theology and our relationship with Christ and is the focus of Days 1-3 in our lesson as we look at what it means for Jesus to be the Way, the Truth, and the Life.

1. What do you think it means when Jesus says that He is *"the way"*? How is that different from saying that He is "a way"? Do you personally believe that Jesus is the only way to the Father and to salvation?

2. We see throughout John that Jesus is the way to the Father (14:6b), the way to eternal life (3:16), the way out of condemnation (3:17), and the way to life (11:25 and 20:31). How would you explain this to someone who isn't a Christian but who is seeking?

3. We can be assured that Jesus longs to actively be *"the way"* in our own personal lives as well. As John 10:3-4 indicates, He calls us each by name and leads us, yes, in the way of salvation, but also in so much more—

everything from the individual plan He has for our lives to details on such things as understanding our children, what we should do with our money, decision making moments, etc. How have you found Jesus to be *"the way"* in your personal life? Can you think of specific examples of how He has led you?

4. What do you think it means when Jesus says He is *"the truth"*? How does this differ from Jesus being "a truth"?

5. One effect of our culture becoming more and more postmodern is the shift from a belief in universal truth to belief that truth is ever-changing and left up to the interpretation of each individual. Unfortunately, some of this has even entered the Christian church. What encouragement and exhortation do you get from the truth that Jesus is *"the truth"*?

6. Knowing Jesus is *"the truth"* is the firm foundation of our faith and gives us validity and motivation in sharing the gospel. John speaks frequently about truth throughout the book, showing us that His truth also affects followers of Christ in a very personal way. Here are some of the instances:

1:14b	Jesus came full of truth
1:17	truth came through Jesus
17:17	the truth sanctifies us
17:17	His word is truth
8:31-32	if we obey his teachings, we will know the truth and the truth will set us free
16:13	the Spirit will guide us into all truth
14:17	the Spirit of truth lives in believers and will be with us forever

As you spend some time with these verses, how do you find they pertain to you? How have you seen God's truth and its effects demonstrated in your life in the ways above?

7. What do you think Jesus means when He says He is *"the life"*?

8. John speaks repeatedly about the life Jesus offers us and, as you know by now, it is a major theme in his gospel. As we speak to seeking hearts around us, we can confidently proclaim that belief in Jesus is the only way to obtain eternal life. Throughout this gospel, however, John also speaks to the richness and fullness of life Jesus offers to believers continually. Here are only a few of the many John and Jesus speak of:

1:4	His life is the light of men
5:39-40	we find life only when we come to Him
6:35	He is the bread of life, those who eat of Him are never hungry again
6:63	the Spirit gives life, His words are life
8:12	if we follow Him, we have the light of life
7:38	streams of living water flow from us
10:10	He has come that we might have life and have it to the full
17:3	Now this is eternal life: that we might know the Father and Jesus the Son
21:30	by believing in Jesus (or continuing to believe) we have life in His name

As you look at your life since becoming a Christian, do any of the above verses resonate with you? How has Jesus brought life to you and how would you describe it? For example, one way to describe the life Jesus has brought me is to liken it to watching "The Wizard of Oz." The film starts out in black and white and all sorts of shades of gray. Then, in a magical moment, color appears, enhancing details, adding richness, depth, and beauty. Jesus has filled my life with color.

9. What things in our world claim to give us life? Compared to the life Jesus gives, how do they fall short?

There may be some who are reading this who believe in Jesus as their Savior, but the concept of Him bringing life in the here and now is foreign. If that sounds like you, ask Jesus to reveal this truth to you. Jesus wants to bring you the fullness of life in so many ways, not just in eternity, but right here, right now.

Days 4-7 John 14:8-15:17 *Key Dynamics of our Relationship with Jesus*

Because there are recurring themes throughout this text, we are going to study the remainder of chapter 14 and all of 15 and 16 as a whole. Jesus explains here how His relationship with His disciples will continue after He leaves them. They have been walking in His presence and following His guidance for three years; the concept of a continuing relationship—much less a *thriving* and *intimate* relationship—without Him present is completely foreign. And so, Jesus beautifully and effectively explains the dynamics of this coming relationship, reinforcing it through the powerful imagery of a vine and its branches. The wonder of God's Word is that the power and truth of Jesus' words transcend time and culture, for it is just as relevant for us today as it was for the 11 disciples on that quiet night before his arrest and crucifixion.

Key Dynamics of a Relationship with Jesus: The Presence of the Holy Spirit, the Value of Obedience, and Asking in Jesus' Name (Days 4-5)

The Presence of the Holy Spirit
To say the Holy Spirit is important in our relationship with Jesus is a gross understatement. It is vital!

1. What do you learn about the Holy Spirit in the following texts:

14:16

How does the Holy Spirit serve as a Counselor?

14:17

What does this mean?

14:23

14:26

What do you think this is referring to?

15:26

16:7

16:12

16:13-15

2. How would you sum up Jesus' teaching on the Holy Spirit in these verses?

3. These verses are not just to be studied with our minds, but were spoken by Jesus to be instilled in our lives. In light of this, what have you personally experienced as you look over these various aspects of the Holy Spirit? What do you desire to experience more of?

The Value of Obedience

According to Jesus, our love for Him is displayed in our obedience.

1. How are love and obedience related according to the following verses? Why do you think this is?

14:15

14:21

14:23

15:10

2. Read John 14:21. What is the connection between obedience and Jesus revealing Himself to us?

3. What kinds of things are we to obey?

4. Obedience is not often easy. What obstacles do you face in obeying Christ?

5. Why do you think obedience is important in our relationship with Christ? How does disobedience hurt it?

a study on devotion to Jesus from the book of john

Asking in Jesus' Name

Jesus clearly and repeatedly communicates that He wants us to ask for things in accordance with His will and that He is eager to answer.

1. What do the following verses teach about asking and the conditions surrounding it?

14:13-14

15:7

15:16

16:24

2. Clearly the texts are not saying that Jesus is like a divine Santa Claus. How would you summarize appropriate asking on our part, Jesus' desire to give, and conditions which allow him to give freely? Does any of this surprise you?

3. What hinders us from receiving what we ask for?

4. In light of all of the above, how would you evaluate how you ask for things from God?

The Vine and the Branches John 15 (Days 6-7)
Jesus reinforces His teaching through this powerful metaphor.

1. Explain the metaphor Jesus uses to effectively communicate a vibrant relationship with Him? Who is the vine? Who are the branches? What is the fruit? Draw it below:

2. Following this metaphor, how do the vine, branch, and fruit work together?

3. What is the key verb in this text that connects the vine to the branch? We will explore this in a moment, but initially, what do you think that means?

4. List below everything associated with *"remaining"* or *"abiding"* according to the text.

5. What are the benefits of abiding according to John 15?

6. The Greek word for *"remain"* is *meno* which holds the notion of staying or remaining with permanence or constancy. The same Greek

word used in John 15 is also used in John 14:16-17 which refers to the Holy Spirit *"dwelling"* in us. Indeed, the concept of *"remain"* in this setting is *a two way concept:* we remain/abide in Christ, Christ remains/abides in us. Jesus remains in us through the Holy Spirit. What do you think helps us, on our end, remain in Jesus?

7. What is essential to bearing fruit? What does fruit look like in our lives? What kind of fruit have you seen God produce in your life?

8. How would you connect the metaphor of the vine and the branches to what we studied earlier in this lesson on the Holy Spirit, obedience/love, and asking/receiving from Jesus?

Days 8–9 *The Cost of Devoted Discipleship - John 15:18-16:4*

1. As we have studied so far in these chapters, the benefits of a relationship with Jesus Christ are many; in fact, we were made for this relationship and thrive when we are in it. However, Jesus makes it clear in this text that there is a cost that comes with a thriving relationship with Him. What should we expect from *"the world"*? Who is *"the world"*?

2. Think back to previous lessons which involved the healing of the man born blind and the raising of Lazarus from the dead. Jesus did a great work in each of their lives and they were devoted followers of Christ. The response of *"the world,"* or of the Pharisees in these cases, was not rational or fair; rather, it was extreme and unjust—the blind man was put out of the synagogue and Lazarus' life was sought after. Because we follow Jesus, we need to expect persecution. In fact, the more we grow in a relationship with Christ, the more likely we will experience it. Why is this do you think?

3. Although the prospect of persecution can threaten to instill fear in us, what encouragement does Jesus offer his disciples and us, as well, in John 16:33? What do you think this verse means?

4. Do you think the future holds more and more persecution of Christians? If so, what do you think it will look like?

5. In a world that is growing increasingly hostile to Christianity, Jesus wants and needs disciples who are ever devoted to Him. If this is your desire, take a moment to share that with Jesus and ask Him to strengthen you for whatever type of persecution might lie ahead of you.

Day 10 Unity in Jesus - John 17

Jesus has finished sharing His heart with His disciples and now is spending intimate time with His Father before His death. As you **read John 17** you will probably see divisions in your Bible with the subheadings: Jesus prays for Himself, Jesus prays for His disciples, Jesus prays for all believers. Let's take a look at these a little more closely.

1. **Jesus Prays for Himself** John 17:1-5. Five times Jesus uses the word *"glory"* or *"glorify"* in these verses. What are the different ways Jesus is glorified or has glory, according to the text?

2. **Jesus Prays for His Disciples** John 17:6-19. Look closely at this text. What does Jesus ask the Father to do for the disciples?

3. **Jesus Prays for All Believers** John 17:20-26. The first part of this prayer communicates a strong theme. What is it?

What encouragement do you get from verses 25-26, knowing that Jesus is referring to you and others who would later believe in Him?

Deepening our Devotion...

"I am the vine; you are the branches. If a man remains in me and I in him, he will bear much fruit; apart from me you can do nothing."
John 15:5

The essence of life in Christ is so succinctly captured in this verse. It is simple, really. Jesus infuses His life into ours with the power of the Holy Spirit and we bear fruit. Apart from Him we do not bear fruit. And what are fruits that a Christian bears? Scripture tells us it is demonstrated in certain attributes from the Spirit (love, joy, peace, patience, kindness, goodness, gentleness, faithfulness, self-control—Galatians 5:22-23), changed lives from our witness and ministry (Romans 1:13), and praising God and thankfully confessing His name (Hebrews 13:15). The Holy Spirit abides in us permanently and we permanently belong to Jesus Christ (remember *meno*?).

Ahh…but if it is so simple, why isn't fruit constantly flowing in our hearts, out of our mouths, and through the work of our hands? Why aren't we clearly discerning His voice and direction all the time? Why do we sometimes feel disconnected from God? Well, there are all kinds of reasons. We know from Scripture, and from just living life on this side of heaven, that life in the here and now is so *unperfect*. Being sinful people living in a sinful world is cumbersome and cloudy. *"Now we see but a poor reflection"* and only *"know in part."* But one day we will *"see face to face"* and *"know fully"* (2 Corinthians 13:12). We are in the in-between-time.

Also, we have to increasingly learn to draw from Him—to open up the avenues in our *"branch"* to receive. This is Christian growth. What does this look like? Well, Jesus tells us. It is things like *obeying* His commands and promptings; *saturating* our minds and hearts with the truth of His word; *asking* for His help, movement, strength, and discernment.

Sometimes this shows itself in little moments, choices, and opportunities. For example, when I realize my mind is burdened with worry, I turn it into prayer; when I realize I am stuck in a problem and am relying on myself to figure it out, I turn my attention to Him and ask for His discernment, strength, words, or whatever it is I need at the moment; when I realize I have yielded to temptation, I say, "Jesus, I am sorry…please help me!" Deepening our relationship with Jesus often occurs in the commonplace of life. Sometimes, though, the issues are bigger and I need to bring them before Jesus as He reveals them to me. Am I living in blatant disobedience to something? That will hinder me. Have I not been spending time in the Word? That will hinder me as well. Am I not asking God to move in a difficult situation? That, too, will limit my bearing fruit. In all these, Jesus does not condemn us in our wanderings and shortcomings, but He does want us to change course when we become aware of it. I believe Jesus delights in small and big decisions we make that open the door to His presence. He loves flowing through our lives!

Take a moment or two to look at your relationship to Christ from the lens of a branch connected to the vine. What do you see in terms of the aspects Jesus encourages you to cultivate in John 14 and 15: asking, obeying, drawing from the Holy Spirit, letting Jesus' words and love abide in you?

a study on devotion to Jesus from the book of john

Life Unending
Lesson 10
John 18,19,20,21

Darkness and death; light and life. Both reach their peak in these final chapters of John. Although Jesus foretold His disciples of His coming death, their world is plunged into darkness as Jesus is taken from them. Indeed, this was humanity's darkest hour as well. As John told us in Chapter 1, however, the darkness has not—and cannot—overcome the light. Victory always belongs to Jesus.

Days 1–2 *Darkness and Death – John 18-19*

1. Read John 18-19. Take some time to prayerfully read and ponder the arrest, trial, and crucifixion of Jesus. Ask the Holy Spirit to speak to you personally in this life changing, world changing, foundational portion of God's purpose and plan. Note below any reflections.

2. Read John 19:30. What did Jesus say and, more importantly, what did He mean by it?

3. If Jesus is all about light and life, why is His death so significant?

Days 3–5 Light and Life – John 20-21

1. Read John 20: 1-15. As you read this text, try to step into the shoes of three different people:

Mary. It is early morning on the third day after Jesus' death. His disciples and other followers are still reeling from the horrors of Friday. In these dark hours, Mary of Magdala—a devoted follower of Jesus whom Jesus had freed of several demons sometime earlier—walks to the tomb, only to discover that Jesus' body is missing. Can you feel her sorrow? How much more can she take...crucifying Jesus is not enough? Now somebody has to steal his body as well?

Peter. It is early morning on the third day following the death of Jesus. Perhaps Peter is still sleeping, but most likely he is tossing and turning—consumed by sorrow, despair, fear, and something else...something else not felt by the others, but which feels like a burden he will never break free from: guilt. Can you feel his torment? Having failed miserably and denying—even to a mere servant girl!—that he knew Jesus...well, how does one recover from that? Suddenly, Mary bursts in the door with even more bad news. Adrenaline kicks in and he dashes to the tomb.

John. John—who calls himself *"the disciple whom Jesus loved"*—is with Peter this early morning, his heart broken with the loss of his best friend and Lord. Suddenly Mary bursts in, clearly distressed, "They have taken the Lord out of the tomb, and we don't know where they have put Him!" Clearly awake now, John joins Peter and rushes to the tomb. A flicker of something—hope?—stirs inside him.

Do any of these perspectives resonate with you?

2. Read John 20:16-20. As you read this text, note how Mary, Peter, and John's world changed in a moment. What do you think each was feeling and thinking?

Mary

Peter

John

Do you think Jesus understands the debilitating effects of fear, guilt, or sorrow? How can the truth of His resurrection dispel them?

3. Read John 20:21-29. Besides the hope of His resurrection, what does Jesus give the disciples? Why was important for them?

The powerful presence of the Holy Spirit was THE key factor in empowering these men to go forward as they built the early church. Knowing Jesus was the Messiah wasn't enough, knowing they had the Truth wasn't enough, memories of their time with Jesus wasn't enough. Though all these things were important, it was only the presence of the Holy Spirit that enabled them to move forward. It is no less important for us as devoted followers of Jesus Christ.

4. Read John 20:24-31. How did Jesus address Thomas' hesitation in this text?

Do you think Jesus was angry that Thomas doubted?

5. Read John 21:1-19. What do you see of Peter's zeal in the first part of this text?

In addition to receiving the Holy Spirit, Peter needed some one-on-one time with Jesus to take care of some issues. This was important before Peter could move forward with confidence. What do you think is going on in these verses?

6. Read John 21:20-25. What is Jesus' correcting comment to Peter in v.22? What lessons can we learn from this?

7. Finally, read John 20:30-31. As we noted at the beginning of this study, John's purpose for writing his gospel is stated here, and is clearly meant for you personally. Before closing out this study on John, take some time to page through this book in your Bible. As you read through the subheadings, note below any specific ways that God has spoken to you through this amazing and God-inspired piece of Scripture. Ask Him to etch these truths into your heart.

Deepening our Devotion...

A closer look at *"In Him was life, and that life was the light of men."*
You John 1:4

If you recall from our very first lesson, the Greek word for *"life"* that John often uses is *zoe*. Its meaning encompasses physical and eternal life, but also the fullness of life as God intended it to be—Holy Spirit given and Holy Spirit empowered—saturating our minds, hearts, and wills. It will last into eternity, but it is also a gift for the here and now.

The gospel of John is an invitation into this life. As we see in this great book, Jesus brought life everywhere He went and to every life He touched. Life radiated from Him because He *was* life. But the present tense is also true: life radiates from Him because He *is* life. Jesus Christ offers life to every fiber of your being and every aspect of your circumstances. He offers life to your gifts, talents, frailties, weaknesses, relationships, and personality. He offers life to the entirety of your past, present, and future. There is no end to it. Even in death, if you belong to Christ, your dying body will be *"swallowed up by life"* (2 Corinthians 5:4). And then? Well, it will be the entrance to the next chapter of life that will never end; life that is more than you could ever ask for or imagine.

This is the life you were destined for. An ordinary person touched by an extraordinary God.

Will you join me, along with John, Peter, the woman at the well, Mary, Lazarus, Nicodemus, the man born blind—and all the others we have met these past few weeks—and respond to this great love with your undivided devotion? If this is your desire, please join me in the following prayer or pray your own prayer of commitment:

Dear Jesus,
Thank you for dying on the cross, for conquering death, and bringing life to all who believe in you. I believe in you with everything in me and offer you my heart and my life in response. I ask that your life reign in me, saturating every part of being—even in ways I don't even realize. I need you and love you. I am yours. May your life in me be my light and the light that shines through me to reach others. Amen.

May God's richest blessing be upon you as you live out the life for which you were destined.

Made in the USA
Lexington, KY
28 December 2015